Contributors

John Keeble
John Bosworth
Jonathan Bockian
Stephen St. Francis Decky
Roger P. Heath
Amelia Sterling
John Talisker
Brendan Corbett
Andrew Bowen
Marin Darmonkow
Paul DeRenzo
Marcel Marquié
Ravi Yaranian
Rick Bohm
Roly Andrews
Ron Ladner
John Keeble
T Geezer
T.D. Amber
T.D. Severin

Review Tales
A Book Magazine For Indie Authors

COPYRIGHT © 2025

Review Tales Magazine - A Book Magazine for Indie Authors

Founder & Editor in Chief: S. Jeyran Main
Publisher: Review Tales Publishing & Editing Services
Print & Distribution: Ingram Spark
Designs: Pexels
ISBN 978-1-988680-98-9 (Paperback)
ISBN 978-1-988680-99-6 (Digital)
www.jeyranmain.com
For all inquiries, please contact us directly.

Photo Credits from Pexels:
pexels-rdne-5530630
pexels-natalie-goodwin-2148267387-32406119
pexels-nietjuhart-29196578
pexels-ebahir-29342340

Editor's Note

As we close out another remarkable year, it is with great excitement that we present the 12th edition of Review Tales. This December issue is a celebration of stories, voices, and the joy of discovering new worlds through books. From tales that warm the heart to narratives that challenge the mind, this edition reflects the diversity, creativity, and passion of today's authors.

The holiday season is often a time of reflection, connection, and gratitude, and in these pages, you'll find works that capture all of that and more. Whether you're seeking inspiration, adventure, or a quiet moment of contemplation, the books featured here offer something special for every reader. It is our hope that these stories spark conversation, invite curiosity, and remind us of the power of storytelling to bring people together— especially in a season centered on shared experiences.

This edition also continues our commitment to highlighting both established voices and emerging authors, providing a platform where every story can find its audience. As always, we are grateful to the authors who entrust us with their work and to the readers who join us in exploring the ever-evolving landscape of literature.

As we move into a new year, we invite both readers and authors to be part of the ongoing conversation. There is still time to feature your work in upcoming issues, and we are always eager to share fresh perspectives, new narratives, and the stories that deserve to be heard.

From all of us at Review Tales, we wish you a joyful holiday season filled with books, discovery, and inspiration. Thank you for celebrating the magic of storytelling with us.

Jeyran Main

Warmly,
Jeyran Main
Editor-in-Chief, Review Tales Magazine

WINTER 2025 | ISSUE 12

BOOK REVIEWS

Review Tales is thrilled to have reached the milestone of over 2000 book reviews. With this extensive experience, we've had the privilege of exploring a vast range of literature. Our reviews are always impartial and thoughtfully crafted to highlight authors' strengths while inspiring them to keep creating. For this Winter issue, we've handpicked exceptional book reviews to feature.

TO APPLY FOR A BOOK REVIEW VISIT
WWW.JEYRANMAIN.COM

Contributors

HONEY TIGERS BY JOHN KEEBLE

CLEO & BESS BY JOHN BOSWORTH

WHAT WAS FORBIDDEN BY JONATHAN BOCKIAN

WEREWOLF MOVIE BY STEPHEN ST. FRANCIS DECKY

WARRIORS OF THE CONTINUUM PART TWO BY ROGER P. HEATH

BREAK FREE FROM NARCISSISTIC ABUSE BY AMELIA STERLING

VILLAGE OF THE GOLDEN GLEAM BY JOHN TALISKER

BLOOD AND FLAME BY BRENDAN CORBETT

ANNE'S FOREVER CHRISTMAS TREE BY ANDREW BOWEN

AL'S JOURNEY BY MARIN DARMONKOW

CALM WITHIN CHAOS BY PAUL DERENZO

PARISIAN DETECTIVE TALES, A TRILOGY BY MARCEL MARQUIÉ

THE COST OF HEALING BY RAVI YARANIAN

SOPHIA'S ABERRANT LEGACY BY RICK BOHM

THE FRONT STEP BY ROLY ANDREWS

SHAGGY'S CHEESEBURGERS BY RON LADNER

A SOCIAL WAR BY SIMON RUMNEY

MIIGIWEWIN: (THE GIFT) BY T GEEZER

SACRED ASHES BY T.D. AMBER

DEADLY VISION BY T.D. SEVERIN

Honey Tigers by John Keeble

John Keeble's Honey Tigers is a hauntingly intelligent and emotionally charged technothriller that explores the thin boundary between humanity and artificial intelligence. Set in a near-future world where corporations manipulate minds for profit, this story feels both futuristic and frighteningly possible. The novel opens with a powerful hook: "First they stole our memories. Then our minds. Now they profit from our pain." From there, the reader is pulled into a world of digital warfare, emotional resilience, and moral questioning.

At the heart of the story are Daisy and Jazon — reluctant heroes — and their six-year-old Honey Tiger, Izzey. Their journey through shifting power dynamics, invisible armies, and coded realities is gripping from start to finish. Keeble crafts their relationship with tenderness, grounding the larger, cerebral themes in human emotion. The contrast between intimate family moments and the vast, impersonal digital battlefield adds depth and urgency to the narrative.

The prose is rich and atmospheric, often echoing the tone of classics like Blade Runner and The Matrix. Yet Keeble gives the genre his own twist — this isn't just about machines or rebellion, but identity, belonging, and survival.

The inclusion of a trans lead character brings fresh representation to science fiction, handled with sincerity and strength. The LGBTQIA+ themes aren't tokenized but woven naturally into the larger questions of transformation and humanity.

While the story unfolds as a slow burn, it rewards patient readers with layered world-building, emotional payoff, and moments of striking philosophical insight. The tension between truth and illusion keeps the reader questioning reality alongside the characters.

Honey Tigers is more than a dystopian adventure; it's a reflection on who we are becoming in an age of algorithms and automation. Thought-provoking, poignant, and chillingly relevant, Keeble's novel lingers long after the final page — a must-read for fans of cyberpunk and speculative fiction.

Cleo & Bess by John Bosworth

John Bosworth's Cleo & Bess: Rivals in Time is a lively and imaginative time-travel adventure that brings two of history's most iconic queens together in a story that is equal parts fun, action, and historical intrigue. Perfectly crafted for younger readers aged 10-14, the novel blends history, fantasy, and humor in a way that educates while it entertains.

The story begins in 1554 with a young Elizabeth Tudor, imprisoned in the Tower of London by her scheming sister, and 1,500 years earlier with a young Cleopatra, exiled and desperate to reclaim her throne. Both girls are trapped in situations that seem hopeless—Elizabeth confined by her family and Cleopatra by the political upheaval of ancient Egypt. Bosworth sets the stage with high stakes, showing the intelligence, courage, and determination that would define these legendary women.

The plot takes a thrilling turn when a mysterious man with an impossible device whisks both girls through time to 1950s Hollywood. Here, Bosworth's storytelling shines, blending historical figures and settings with playful modern adventures. Cleopatra and Elizabeth navigate airplanes, jeeps, department stores, and the glamour of the silver screen, creating humorous and engaging scenarios that young readers will adore. The contrast between ancient queens and mid-20th-century America is both amusing and insightful, emphasizing how these characters adapt, learn, and grow when faced with unfamiliar worlds.

But the story is not just about fun adventures. Cleopatra's ambition soon drives her to manipulate history itself, aiming to rule Ancient Egypt, Ancient Rome, and even modern America.

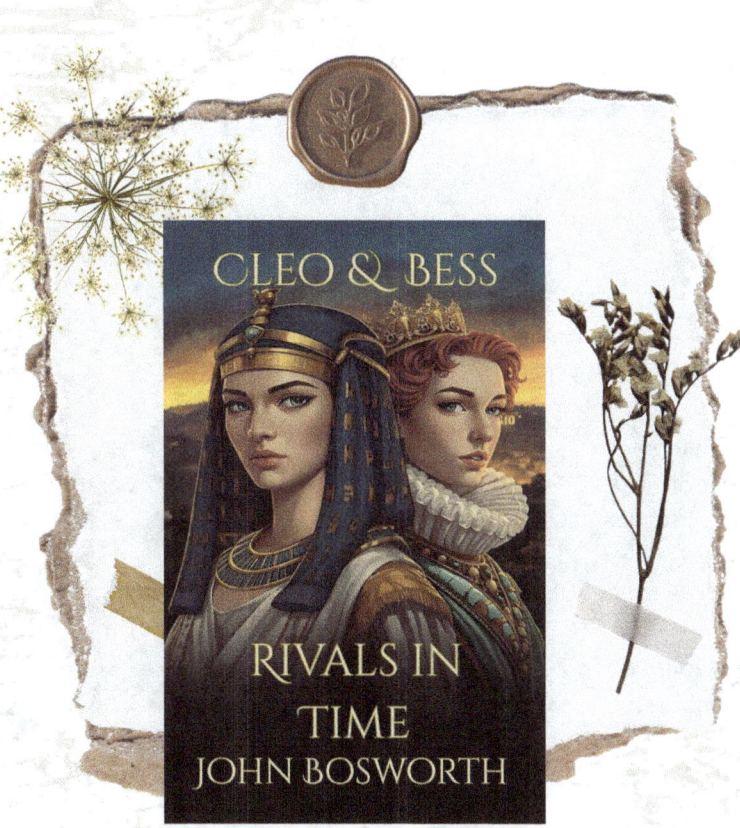

Elizabeth must find a way to stop her friend before she reshapes the past and future, creating tension and moral lessons about responsibility, friendship, and the consequences of unchecked ambition. The interplay between loyalty and competition gives the story emotional depth while maintaining a fast-paced, engaging narrative.

From the Tower of London to the Hollywood Hills, from ancient Alexandria to a futuristic planet, Bosworth's writing is vivid, playful, and accessible, offering readers both adventure and a creative look at history. The novel balances humor, suspense, and educational value, encouraging curiosity about the past while exploring timeless themes of leadership, courage, and friendship.

Cleo & Bess: Rivals in Time is a fun, inspiring, and action-packed tale that will delight young readers and spark their imagination. Bosworth successfully merges history with fantasy, creating a story where legends aren't just born —they create each other.

What Was Forbidden by Jonathan Bockian

Jonathan Bockian's What Was Forbidden is an elegantly crafted and emotionally resonant historical novel that plunges readers into the heart of 17th-century Venice — a city shimmering with beauty yet shadowed by confinement. Set in 1672, the story unfolds within the Jewish Ghetto, a walled quarter where faith and identity are tightly policed. Against this backdrop, a single tragedy sets everything in motion: the brutal murder of Mordechai, a restless merchant and skeptic who quietly rebelled against the world he was born into.

At the center stands Yehudit, Mordechai's devoted sister, whose grief ignites a relentless search for truth. As she retraces the final days of her brother's life, she is forced to confront not only what happened to him, but also the rigid structures that bind her own existence.

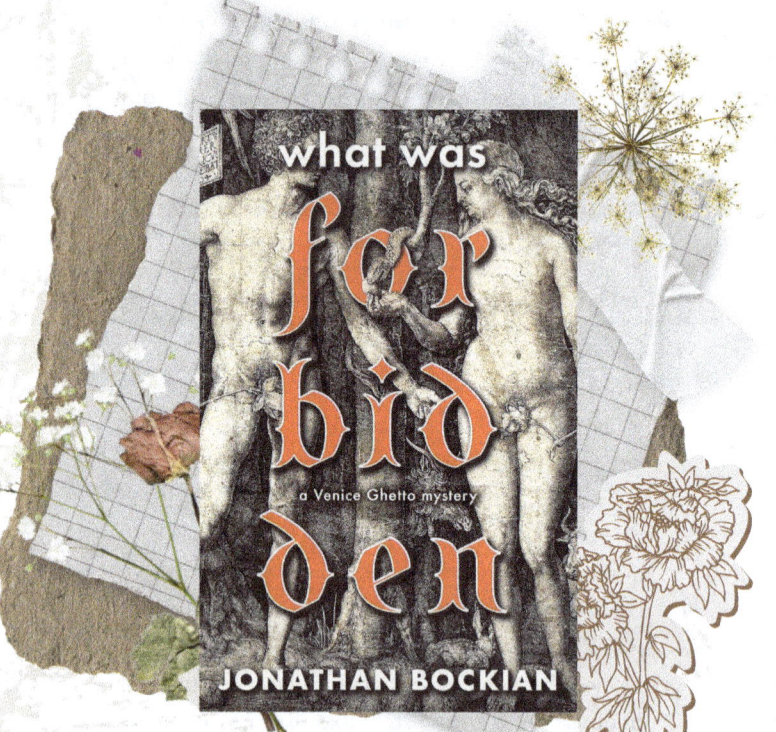

Yehudit's journey becomes a layered exploration of justice, womanhood, and freedom — a defiance of both the patriarchal confines of her faith and the oppressive Christian world that encircles it.

Bockian's prose is lyrical yet disciplined, vividly evoking the sounds, scents, and moral tensions of Venetian life. The Ghetto is not simply a setting but a living character — a place of intellect, devotion, commerce, and quiet despair. Through intimate detail and careful pacing, Bockian portrays the intersection of theology, philosophy, and human emotion, allowing readers to feel the suffocating walls of the Ghetto even as Yehudit pushes against them.

What makes What Was Forbidden especially compelling is its moral complexity. There are no simple villains or saints; every act of rebellion and silence carries consequence.

Bockian examines the clash between faith and autonomy with nuance, never reducing the story to mere historical commentary. The novel's themes — censorship, gender roles, and the courage to speak forbidden truths — echo powerfully in the modern world, reminding us that the fight for freedom of conscience is timeless.

What Was Forbidden is not only a mystery but a meditation on integrity and resistance. It's about the cost of truth and the quiet heroism of those who refuse to be silenced. With its richly drawn characters, emotional depth, and moral clarity, Jonathan Bockian's novel stands out as a beautifully written and profoundly human work of historical fiction.

Werewolf Movie by Stephen St. Francis Decky

Stephen St. Francis Decky's Werewolf Movie is a masterful blend of horror, surrealism, and dark humor that explores friendship, creativity, and the unpredictable forces that shape life. Set in South Jersey during the late 1980s, the story follows four friends working dead-end jobs who find meaning and purpose in the South Jersey/Philadelphia music scene. Decky captures the energy, ambition, and camaraderie of youth, showing how music and artistic expression serve as both refuge and a catalyst for personal growth.

The story quickly moves from the mundane to the extraordinary. Following a couple of unexpected deaths, a chance encounter with a mysterious record label executive sends the group into a hallucinatory spiral where reality and illusion blur. Strange and terrifying events begin to occur: poltergeist activity, savage claw marks appearing on vehicles, and unexplained bloody injuries unsettle both the characters and the reader. Decky expertly balances horror with humor, creating moments that are both shocking and darkly absurd, making the story unpredictable and compelling.

Told from the first-person perspectives of each of the four friends, the novel allows readers to enter the minds of its central characters, offering a deep understanding of their fears, motivations, and moral struggles. This narrative approach emphasizes the psychological impact of extraordinary events, highlighting the tension between choice and circumstance. As the friends confront ethical dilemmas and external threats, Decky explores themes of agency, loyalty, and personal responsibility. The moral complexity adds layers to the story, elevating it beyond a traditional horror tale.

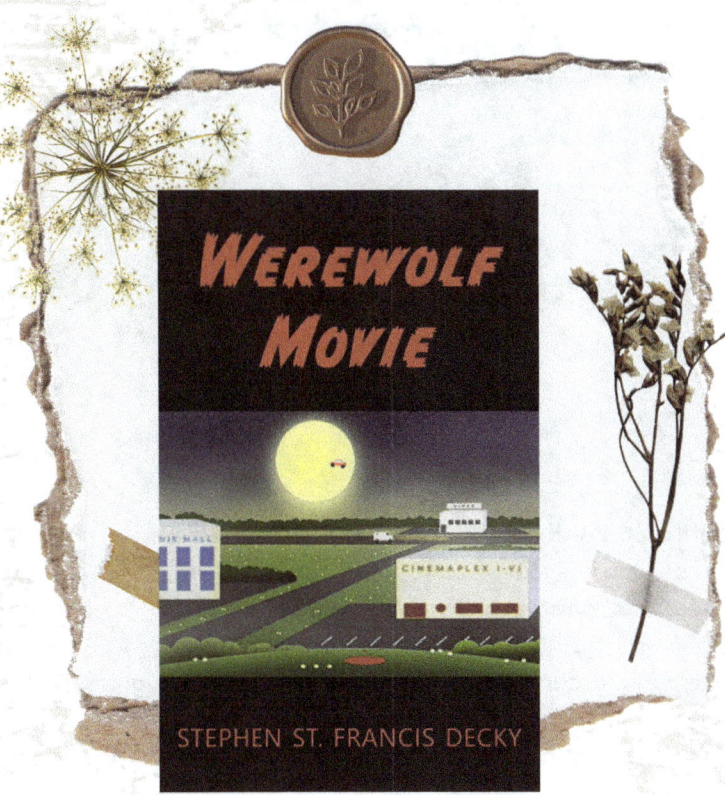

At its core, Werewolf Movie is also a meditation on the ferocity and urgency of creativity. Decky examines the music industry's predatory aspects, showing how ambition, exploitation, and competition shape the lives of aspiring artists. The hallucinatory events mirror these pressures, reflecting the characters' internal struggles alongside the external chaos they face. This blend of surrealism, psychological insight, and social commentary makes the novel both engaging and thought-provoking.

Decky's prose is vivid, sharp, and immersive. The late-1980s setting comes alive with cultural references, music, and authentic dialogue, grounding the supernatural elements in a realistic world. The balance of suspense, humor, and horror keeps readers invested, while the story's unpredictable twists maintain tension throughout.

Werewolf Movie is a multifaceted reading experience, perfect for fans of horror with psychological depth, surreal storytelling, or tales of friendship tested by extraordinary circumstances. Decky crafts a narrative that is thrilling, emotionally resonant, and intellectually engaging, making the novel a standout exploration of creativity, morality, and the thin line between reality and the uncanny.

Warriors of the Continuum Part Two by Roger P. Heath

In Warriors of the Continuum Part Two: Deception, Roger P. Heath delivers a compelling and immersive sequel that deepens the complexity of his fantasy universe. Picking up where the first installment left off, the story expands in scope, tension, and moral ambiguity, challenging readers to question loyalty, truth, and the line between light and shadow.

The reluctant Warriors are hounded by the followers of Kaos, the god of the Dark, as they strive to protect the Iyes tribe. Amidst their struggle, they seek answers about the Ka, the Kade, and the looming threat of the Geddon, the Land's Armageddon. Heath keeps readers on edge, revealing secrets and conspiracies in a world where prophecy, power, and ancient forces collide. The title Deception resonates throughout the novel, as nearly every character hides truths, creating layers of intrigue and uncertainty that drive the story forward.

Warriors of the Continuum
Part Two

DECEPTION

Roger P. Heath

Central to the narrative is the haunting guidance of IY, god of the Light: "Fighters on the battlefield will not win this war." This warning underscores the novel's deeper theme—that victory may require wisdom, collaboration, and sacrifice, not just strength. Heath uses this moral tension to explore human nature, trust, and the cost of deception, giving the story a philosophical and emotional weight beyond standard fantasy conflict.

Heath's prose is vivid and immersive. The harsh, sacred landscapes mirror the characters' inner struggles, while the mythic tone of the storytelling lends grandeur to the narrative. The interplay of spiritual forces, divine intervention, and personal agency keeps the reader invested in both the characters' fates and the unfolding mysteries of the Continuum.

As the middle book in a trilogy, Deception succeeds in raising the stakes, expanding the world, and leaving enough unanswered to make the final installment urgent and highly anticipated. Fans of high fantasy, morally complex characters, and intricately plotted adventures will find this sequel engaging and rewarding.

Roger P. Heath has crafted a story that balances suspense, depth, and imagination, making Warriors of the Continuum Part Two: Deception a standout entry in epic fantasy.

Break Free from Narcissistic Abuse by Amelia Sterling

Amelia Sterling's Break Free from Narcissistic Abuse is a compassionate and practical guide for anyone seeking to reclaim their life after toxic relationships. Drawing from personal experience and deep understanding, Sterling offers a roadmap to recognize, navigate, and heal from the subtle and destructive patterns of narcissistic abuse. Her narrative combines real-life anecdotes, actionable strategies, and reflective exercises to help readers regain confidence, self-respect, and emotional freedom.

The book opens with Sterling's own story—a candid account of the confusion, self-doubt, and emotional pain that accompany entanglement with a narcissist. By sharing her journey, she immediately establishes empathy and credibility, showing that recovery is possible and that readers are not alone. She carefully explores narcissistic dynamics, emphasizing that narcissism is more than arrogance or vanity. Behaviors like lack of empathy, manipulation, and a constant need for control gradually erode the victim's self-worth, leaving them questioning themselves and their reality.

Sterling's guide is structured to be both informative and actionable. She helps readers identify the subtle and overt signs of narcissistic behavior in partners, family members, or close acquaintances. She also addresses the difficult decision of whether to leave or navigate a relationship with healthier boundaries, emphasizing that there is no one-size-fits-all solution. Instead, she equips readers with tools to make informed choices that align with their well-being.

A central theme is self-care and restoration. Sterling emphasizes rebuilding self-esteem, practicing self-compassion, and prioritizing one's own needs. Through practical exercises, readers can reconnect with their inner strength, develop resilience, and establish firm boundaries. Reflective prompts encourage introspection, helping readers process experiences and gain clarity about their next steps.

What sets this book apart is its blend of psychological insight and hope. Sterling balances understanding the pain of narcissistic abuse with actionable strategies for recovery, demonstrating that healing is achievable and that a fulfilling life beyond abuse is possible. Her compassionate tone and practical guidance empower readers to reclaim autonomy and embrace a future grounded in authenticity, peace, and joy.

Break Free from Narcissistic Abuse is more than a self-help book—it is a beacon of support, a guide to emotional liberation, and a call to reclaim one's inherent worth. For anyone navigating toxic relationships or seeking tools to restore confidence and inner peace, Sterling's work provides clarity, hope, and practical steps toward true recovery.

Village of the Golden Gleam
By John Talisker

John Talisker's Village of the Golden Gleam is a beautifully written, imaginative novel that blends whimsy, wit, and deep reflection in a story that feels both otherworldly and intimately human. The tale transports readers to a paradise-like village inhabited by non-human beings who live in harmony, surrounded by good cheer, innocence, and light. But beneath the idyllic surface, Talisker weaves an undercurrent of tension — a paradise on the brink of change and possible collapse.

The novel follows a courageous group of alien inhabitants who, faced with the disintegration of their utopian world, embark on an extraordinary journey to Earth. Having lived peacefully for centuries, they must now adapt to a new and unfamiliar reality, transforming themselves to survive in a world that is, in many ways, more fragile and flawed than the one they left behind.

Village
of the
Golden Gleam

Life, what is it but a dream?

a novel by
John Talisker

What follows is a thoughtful and heartwarming exploration of identity, adaptation, and the enduring search for meaning and connection. Talisker's writing is both humorous and lyrical, balancing levity with quiet philosophical depth. Through his vivid worldbuilding and endearing characters, he explores profound themes of love, loss, transformation, and the impermanence of all things. The novel also touches on timely questions about technology and artificial intelligence, drawing subtle parallels to the ways modern societies grapple with the consequences of progress and the erosion of innocence.

What makes Village of the Golden Gleam particularly enchanting is its tone — it is playful and strange, yet suffused with wisdom. Readers will find echoes of classic speculative fiction, reminiscent of Ursula K. Le Guin's contemplative storytelling and the gentle absurdity of Douglas Adams, yet the voice remains distinctly Talisker's.

Village of the Golden Gleam is a story about what it means to be alive — to care, to lose, to change, and to hope again. It's a fantasy that lingers in the mind long after the final page, offering a mirror through which we can glimpse our own humanity, seen from the eyes of beings who are not quite human at all.

A remarkable, thought-provoking, and tender novel — both timeless and timely — Village of the Golden Gleam invites readers to dream, to feel, and to reflect on the golden gleam within us all.

Blood and Flame by Brendan Corbett

Brendan Corbett's Blood and Flame is an engaging and immersive fantasy that introduces readers to the Quinarium, a richly built magical society where faith, power, and morality collide. The first book in The Quinate's Faithful series blends high-stakes adventure, moral complexity, and strong character development to create a story that is both thrilling and thought-provoking.

The novel begins with candidates preparing for the Rite of the Faithful, the first step in becoming mages of the Quinarium. Dara, a Blood Mage from humble origins, and Wynne, a Flame Mage from a noble lineage, are paired on a quest to investigate mysterious livestock killings and uncover a rumored mana source. Through their backstories, Corbett establishes characters who are relatable, driven, and morally nuanced, immediately drawing readers into their struggles and growth.

The story unfolds with tension and adventure, as Dara and Wynne face ogres, jackals, and the magical Fae inhabitants of the Nomridian Forest. Paladin Trainee Caudro and Fae Mage Ami provide guidance, but danger is constant, and the challenges test both skill and judgment. The narrative moves seamlessly between action, political intrigue, and moral dilemmas, revealing dark secrets of the Quinarium—including false-flag plots, genocide, and cruel mana-harvesting practices.

Corbett's worldbuilding is detailed and vivid, from the forested lands of the Fae to the treacherous Zanerian Archipelago, creating a sense of wonder and peril. The relationships, particularly between Dara and Wynne, add emotional depth, balancing high-stakes action with tender moments of connection and growing affection. Their bond develops naturally, even as their faith in the Quinarium falters.

By the end of the novel, Dara and Wynne join the enigmatic Imreia, a heretic of the Quinarium, in opposition to the corrupt system, setting the stage for future installments. Blood and Flame is an exciting, morally complex fantasy that combines adventure, intrigue, and strong character arcs.

For readers who enjoy action-packed fantasy with ethical depth, political intrigue, and compelling characters, Blood and Flame is a gripping introduction to a series that promises both adventure and thoughtful exploration of power and faith.

Anne's Forever Christmas Tree
by Andrew Bowen

In Anne's Forever Christmas Tree, author Andrew Bowen delivers a heartfelt and imaginative holiday story that captures the wonder of Christmas, the warmth of family, and the timeless message of kindness that carries far beyond the festive season.

The story begins when a fir tree, destined to become the family's Christmas centerpiece, is struck by a soft, mysterious blue bolt of lightning. This magical spark gives her extraordinary powers and a voice of her own. Named Chris by the family's Irish Setter, Lucky, the two form an unlikely but endearing duo who work quietly behind the scenes to bring joy, safety, and miracles to the household.

Throughout the tale, Bowen beautifully blends whimsy with moral depth. In one memorable scene, Chris and Lucky foil a burglar attempting to steal the family's Christmas presents, saving the holiday through courage and cleverness. In another, they protect a young mother and her baby during an ice storm, keeping them warm and safe until the family returns. These moments shine with compassion and selflessness, showing how magic can dwell in acts of love and bravery.

When Christmas ends, the family follows a southern tradition by planting Chris in their garden. There, she faces teasing from the other trees until she shares her adventures, earning their respect and admiration. The story culminates in a breathtaking scene where Chris is lifted by a wild windstorm, scattering her seeds across the world — ensuring her spirit and kindness live on through countless new fir trees.

Filled with warmth, imagination, and heart, Anne's Forever Christmas Tree is more than a holiday tale — it's a story about legacy, friendship, and the enduring power of love. With gentle, expressive prose and Sue Lynn Cotton's beautifully detailed illustrations, Andrew Bowen brings to life a world where kindness and courage shine brightly, even in the quietest moments. His storytelling captures the wonder of childhood, the magic of the season, and the timeless truth that love, once planted, continues to grow. Thoughtful, uplifting, and deeply touching, this is a modern Christmas classic destined to delight readers of all ages.

Al's Journey
By Marin Darmonkow

Marin Darmonkow's Al's Journey: The Night Everything Changed is a touching and imaginative children's tale that captures the mystery, beauty, and growing pains of self-discovery. Told with the rhythm of a timeless fable, the story follows Al, a young orphan raised by his wise grandfather—the shaman of a gold-obsessed tribe that has lost sight of life's true treasures. When his grandfather reaches his hundredth birthday, he sends Al on a journey up a sacred mountain—a journey that will change him forever.

Guided by glowing fireflies and the quiet voice of courage, Al faces a series of challenges that test his resolve, compassion, and understanding of the world. At the summit, he comes face to face with the divine and asks profound questions about purpose and existence.

The experience transforms him—body, mind, and spirit—into the healer his people so desperately need. Through this gentle metamorphosis, Darmonkow reminds readers that true growth is not about age, but about wisdom, empathy, and learning to see beyond oneself.

The story's strength lies in its simplicity and universality. Children will be drawn to the dreamlike adventure, while adults will find deeper meaning in its allegorical layers. Darmonkow's lyrical writing and luminous illustrations bring the world of Al to life with warmth and wonder. The imagery—fireflies dancing in the dark, the sacred hut on the mountaintop, the golden obsession of the tribe—lingers long after the final page.

At its heart, Al's Journey is about growing up—not just physically, but emotionally and spiritually. It encourages readers, young and old, to ask their own "crucial questions" about who they are and what truly matters. With themes of courage, identity, and transformation, it becomes more than a bedtime story; it's a parable of becoming.

Beautifully written and visually enchanting, Al's Journey: The Night Everything Changed stands out as a modern classic in children's literature—a magical, meaningful tale that teaches the importance of curiosity, compassion, and inner strength. A story to be cherished, discussed, and remembered for generations.

Calm Within Chaos by Paul DeRenzo

Paul DeRenzo's Calm Within Chaos is a compassionate and scientifically grounded guide that meets teens exactly where they are—in the middle of an age defined by pressure, uncertainty, and constant connection. In a world where social media amplifies both connection and comparison, and academic and social demands never seem to pause, DeRenzo offers a practical roadmap for building resilience and emotional balance.

Drawing on years of conversations with teens, educators, and mental health professionals, Calm Within Chaos transforms overwhelming emotional experiences into opportunities for understanding and growth. It blends science-backed insight with real-world application, helping teens make sense of their emotions instead of being controlled by them. Through relatable examples, guided reflections, and 10 hands-on "Teen Inner Peace Challenges," readers are encouraged to take small, consistent steps toward calm, confidence, and self-awareness.

Unlike many self-help books that stay abstract, this one is refreshingly actionable. Each chapter ends with a 7-day challenge designed to bring the lessons off the page and into daily life—helping teens manage conflict, navigate friendships, improve focus, and develop mindful habits that last.

Parents and caregivers will also find valuable tools to start meaningful conversations and provide steady emotional support without judgment or pressure.

DeRenzo's approach is both empathetic and empowering. He doesn't minimize the intensity of teen emotions but instead validates them, guiding readers toward mastery through understanding. By blending the latest psychological research with accessible language, he creates a bridge between emotional awareness and real-life resilience.

Calm Within Chaos stands out as a comprehensive, heartfelt companion for today's youth—a book that reminds teens they are not alone in their struggles and that calm is not the absence of chaos but the strength to face it. For anyone seeking lasting emotional balance, this is more than a guide—it's a lifeline.

Parisian Detective Tales, a Trilogy
By Marcel Marquié

In Parisian Detective Tales: The Child, Marcel Marquié continues his hauntingly evocative trilogy set in postwar France, seamlessly weaving historical intrigue with deeply human emotion. Picking up after the gripping events of Two Sisters, the novel draws readers into a world still shadowed by the trauma of World War II—where guilt, loss, and the desire for redemption linger like ghosts in the streets of Paris.

At its heart lies a mother's enduring agony and a detective's quiet determination. Sandrine, one of the two sisters from the first installment, is haunted by the abduction of her infant son—fathered by a German officer during the war and lost amid the chaos of revenge and retribution. Private investigator Toni Bonnet takes up the search, following faint traces of the child's existence through a labyrinth of deception, secrecy, and wartime scars that refuse to heal.

Marquié's narrative expands beyond Paris, leading Bonnet into the rugged landscapes of the Pyrenees, where remnants of another conflict—the Spanish Civil War—cast long, sorrowful shadows. There, exiled Spanish Republicans and remnants of the Résistance intersect, their fates tangled in questions of loyalty, morality, and survival.

What makes The Child so compelling is Marquié's ability to blend mystery with moral reflection. Every clue uncovered feels weighted with history, every silence heavy with unspoken pain. The prose carries a quiet melancholy, painting the postwar years with both tenderness and truth. Readers of historical fiction will appreciate the intricate period detail, while fans of detective stories will find satisfaction in Bonnet's dogged pursuit of justice—driven not by ambition, but by empathy.

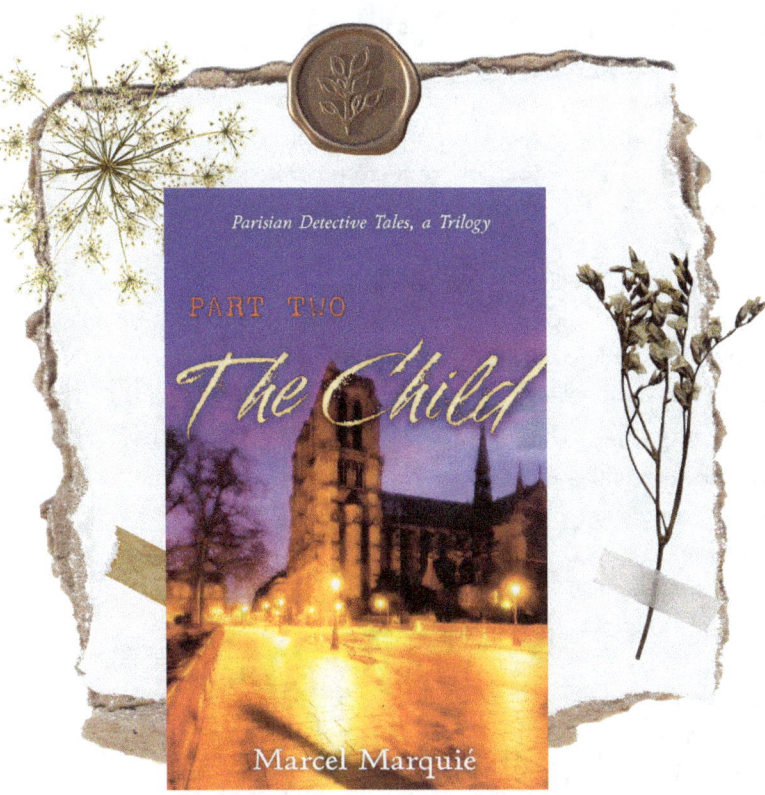

With its seamless fusion of suspense, history, and humanity, The Child stands as a poignant continuation of Marquié's trilogy. It captures not only the aftermath of war but also the fragile hope that persists in its wake. Thoughtful, atmospheric, and deeply moving, this novel reaffirms Marquié's place as a storyteller who understands that every mystery is, ultimately, a story about the human heart. Through Toni Bonnet's relentless search, readers are reminded that even in the ruins of conflict, compassion can illuminate the darkest corners of the past. Marquié leaves us contemplating how love, loss, and the pursuit of truth intertwine to shape the meaning of redemption itself.

15

The Cost of Healing by Ravi Yaranian

Ravi Yaranian's The Cost of Healing is not just a novel—it's a quiet, luminous meditation on the invisible weight of compassion and the courage it takes to reclaim one's own peace. Told through the life of Elera, a gifted healer whose touch restores others at the expense of her own spirit, the book becomes both a mirror and a balm for anyone who has ever loved too much, given too freely, or forgotten themselves in the act of caring for others.

At its heart, The Cost of Healing is a story about boundaries—about what happens when empathy turns into erosion, and when the desire to mend others conceals one's own fractures. Yaranian writes with haunting lyricism and remarkable psychological depth, transforming Elera's supernatural gift into an allegory for emotional labor, burnout, and the cost of unhealed wounds. Her journey from self-sacrifice to self-acceptance unfolds with honesty and tenderness, resonating deeply in a world where strength is often mistaken for endless endurance.

Yaranian's prose feels almost meditative, moving between stillness and revelation with poetic rhythm. Every chapter invites readers to pause, reflect, and breathe—to recognize that healing is neither linear nor painless, but it is always possible. Themes of spiritual renewal, somatic awareness, and emotional authenticity intertwine, offering a nuanced exploration of what it means to be whole after being broken.

Equally striking is how the novel bridges fiction and therapy, functioning as both a story and a companion for self-discovery. Readers who have experienced loss, caregiving fatigue, or emotional numbness will find themselves gently guided toward recognition and release. This is a rare novel that teaches without preaching and heals without pretending to have all the answers.

The Cost of Healing is a tender, transformative work—a hymn to self-compassion and the radical act of resting without guilt. For fans of The Midnight Library and It Ends With Us, Yaranian offers a deeply human reminder: sometimes, the most powerful form of healing begins when you finally choose yourself.

16

Sophia's Aberrant Legacy
By Rick Bohm

Rick Bohm's Sophia's Aberrant Legacy is a compelling and imaginative science-fiction audiobook that explores humanity, morality, and the consequences of unchecked technological power. Narrated through virtual voice, this unabridged audiobook brings the futuristic world to life in a unique and immersive way, capturing both the scope of its society and the intimate journey of its central character, Sophia.

Sophia is introduced as a young woman with mysterious origins, her innocence and purity concealing a profound purpose that resonates across time. Her message is simple and hopeful, a beacon meant to inspire and guide, yet over the course of the story, it becomes corrupted by human arrogance, selfish desires, and the complexities of societal ambition. Through Sophia, Bohm examines how even the purest intentions can be twisted when filtered through human weakness, ambition, or misunderstanding.

The novel's worldbuilding is intricate and thought-provoking. Set in a far-future society, Bohm juxtaposes an advanced technological civilization with communities that embrace simpler, more grounded ways of living. This contrast serves as the backdrop for the central conflict: a growing confrontation between innovation and tradition, power and simplicity, ambition and morality. As the story unfolds, readers encounter a society wrestling with the ethics of intelligence, control, and belief systems, where the very concept of intelligent life is manipulated by those in power.

Bohm's narrative spans generations, evolving from Sophia's initial mission into a sweeping saga marked by hope, greed, and misplaced trust. The story challenges readers to consider the consequences of human ambition, the fragility of morality, and the enduring need for wisdom across time. Sophia's journey is both personal and symbolic—an exploration of purpose, responsibility, and the enduring impact of one individual on an entire civilization.

The use of virtual voice narration adds an extra layer of engagement, giving the audiobook a futuristic, almost otherworldly tone that complements the story's themes of advanced technology and societal evolution. The narration helps immerse listeners in the far-future setting while maintaining clarity and emotional depth in Sophia's journey.

Sophia's Aberrant Legacy is more than a science-fiction tale; it is a meditation on ethics, purpose, and the human heart. Bohm challenges readers to think critically about the choices societies make, the consequences of misplaced ambition, and the power of individual influence. This audiobook is a captivating, thoughtful, and imaginative journey that will appeal to fans of science fiction with moral and philosophical depth, as well as those seeking a story that blends futuristic adventure with profound human insight.

The Front Step
By Roly Andrews

In The Front Step, Roly Andrews crafts a vibrant and eclectic world through thirty short stories that brim with wit, insight, and emotional resonance. Twenty-one of these stories were previously published across global platforms, while nine are entirely new, giving both returning readers and newcomers something fresh to enjoy. Andrews demonstrates a remarkable ability to combine humor and heart, delivering narratives that are as thought-provoking as they are entertaining.

Each story stands alone, yet together they form a rich mosaic of human experience. Some stories lean into the absurd, offering unexpected twists that delight and surprise, while others gently probe the emotional core of everyday life.

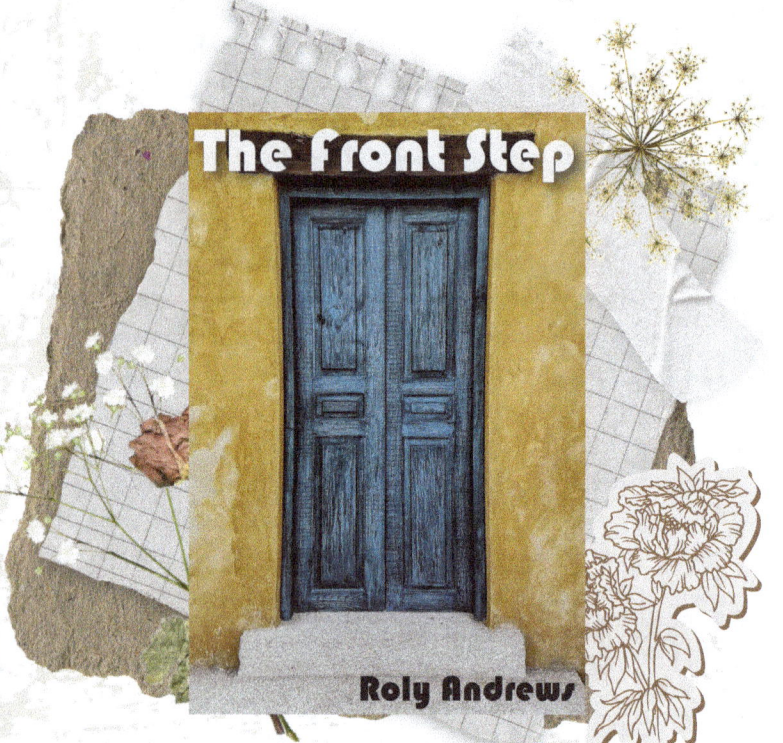

Andrews' voice is distinct—playful yet compassionate, daring yet grounded—and he isn't afraid to break conventional storytelling rules in service of deeper truth. The result is a collection that keeps readers engaged and curious, turning even ordinary moments into reflections worth savoring.

What elevates The Front Step beyond typical short story collections is the author's empathy, informed by his real-life experiences mentoring rough sleepers and advocating for people affected by trauma and disability. This compassion imbues his characters with authenticity, making even the quirkiest or most unconventional moments feel profoundly human. Readers encounter a mix of humor, heartbreak, and hope, discovering stories that linger long after the pages are closed.

The collection also benefits from professional editing and wide-format availability, making it accessible to a broad audience and ensuring a polished, enjoyable reading experience. Whether you are a devoted fan of short fiction or someone seeking fresh literary perspectives, The Front Step offers a rare combination of perspective, joy, and literary magic.

Roly Andrews has produced a work that entertains while touching the heart. The Front Step is a collection that invites readers to pause, reflect, and smile at the small, extraordinary moments of life. It is a book to revisit, savor, and share—a testament to storytelling that celebrates empathy, creativity, and the unpredictable beauty of human experience.

Shaggy's Cheeseburgers by Ron Ladner

In Shaggy's Cheeseburgers, Ron Ladner offers readers a heartfelt memoir that goes beyond entrepreneurship, presenting a story of resilience, community, and the extraordinary power of hope. Set against the backdrop of the Mississippi Gulf Coast, the book chronicles how Ladner lost everything during Hurricane Katrina and then rebuilt not just his life, but a community, through a simple but iconic restaurant: Shaggy's.

Ladner's narrative is infused with warmth, humor, and honesty. From his childhood adventures along the Gulf Coast to the harrowing aftermath of Katrina, he paints a vivid picture of a world devastated by disaster yet brimming with potential for renewal. The story isn't simply about business—it's about the human capacity to overcome adversity, transform tragedy into opportunity, and create meaningful connections along the way.

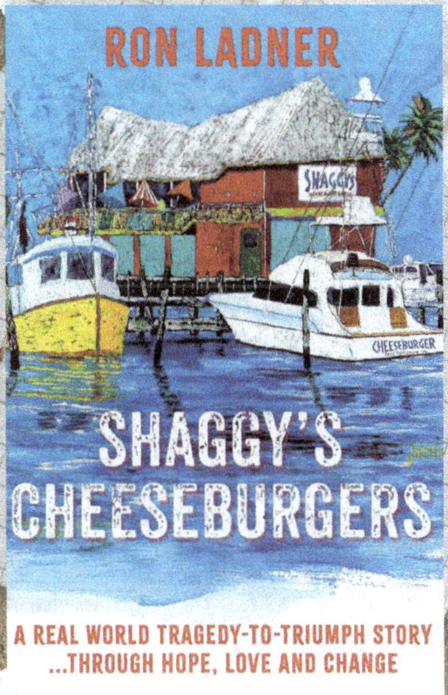

Shaggy's Cheeseburgers serves multiple purposes. It's a memoir of personal growth, a blueprint for building a people-focused business, and a love letter to a community that refused to be defeated. Ladner demonstrates how leadership rooted in empathy and service can inspire both employees and patrons, making a restaurant a true hub of hope and joy. He explores lessons in turning loss into opportunity, creating a culture that values people above profits, and discovering purpose in serving others.

What makes this book particularly compelling are the candid testimonials from Shaggy's team members and local residents, whose lives were touched by the restaurant. These voices reinforce the impact of Ladner's vision and show how one person's perseverance can ripple outward, shaping the lives of many.

Readers who enjoy inspirational business stories like Shoe Dog, Kitchen Confidential, or A Pirate Looks at Fifty will find Shaggy's Cheeseburgers equally engaging, but it's also for anyone seeking motivation, hope, and a reminder that extraordinary outcomes often grow from the simplest beginnings. Ladner proves that sometimes the most profound lessons in life, leadership, and love can come wrapped in a perfectly crafted cheeseburger shared with those who matter most.

This is a story of triumph that leaves readers inspired, uplifted, and reminded of the power of community, resilience, and unwavering optimism.

A Social War by Simon Rumney

Simon Rumney's A Social War is a gripping historical novel that delves deep into the turbulent final days of the Roman Republic through the eyes of a complex and compelling protagonist, Helena. Born into a harsh peasant life among the olive groves, Helena's early experiences of psychological abuse shape her resilience, cunning, and drive for survival. Her journey from slavery to power is as dark as it is fascinating, drawing readers into a vivid and morally complex world.

Helena's intelligence and resourcefulness are recognized by Demophon, Sulla's ailing spymaster, who trains her to serve as his eyes and ears in Rome. This mentorship introduces Helena to a world of political intrigue, espionage, and manipulation. Rumney's portrayal of Helena is nuanced—she is both sympathetic and flawed, a character driven by vengeance and self-preservation, yet constantly grappling with self-doubt and moral compromise.

The story is set against the backdrop of Rome's civil unrest, with Helena maneuvering through a dangerous political landscape. The narrative illustrates the human cost of ambition and the destructive potential of unchecked power.

Helena's calculated schemes to amass wealth and influence eventually spiral out of control, culminating in events that accelerate the violent downfall of the Republic and the rise of the Empire. Rumney captures both the grandeur of Rome and the intimate struggles of his characters with equal skill.

One of the novel's strengths lies in its psychological depth. Helena's internal battles—her addiction, guilt, and self-loathing—add layers of realism to her otherwise strategic and ruthless persona. Readers witness her triumphs and failures, making her journey a cautionary tale about ambition, revenge, and the consequences of moral compromise.

A Social War is perfect for fans of historical fiction, political intrigue, and character-driven narratives. Rumney combines meticulous historical research with a strong, emotionally charged story, bringing to life the complexities of Rome and the extraordinary journey of a young woman navigating a world filled with danger, power, and betrayal. This is a story of resilience, moral conflict, and the transformative, often destructive, nature of ambition.

Miigiwewin: (The Gift)
By T Geezer

T Geezer's Miigiwewin: (The Gift) is an intricately woven, thought-provoking novel that challenges readers to engage deeply with its layered narrative and multifaceted characters. The story begins and ends with the mysterious death of Professor Jason Abram, a charismatic yet enigmatic figure who arrives at the University seeking the inaugural directorship of a new Scholars' Program. Using the promise of grant funding, he persuades the dean to appoint him, setting the stage for a story rich with ambition, transformation, and intellectual intrigue.

While Abram's fate frames the novel, the plot centers on Joyce Robertson's emancipation and the journeys of the students under Abram's guidance. As the narrative unfolds, readers are drawn into a series of events within H.G. Wells Hall, where each character undergoes profound metamorphosis. From their initial uncertainties to the culmination of the Regents' meeting, Geezer masterfully portrays the evolution of these young scholars, demonstrating how circumstances, mentorship, and personal insight shape identity and purpose.

What makes Miigiwewin especially compelling is its careful balance between mystery and philosophical exploration. The novel provides subtle clues while also presenting red herrings, but it is not a conventional "whodunit." Instead, it offers an upmarket literary experience—an intellectual puzzle that encourages readers to consider deeper questions about ambition, growth, and the human condition. Each subplot and character interaction builds toward the ultimate revelation, rewarding attentive readers with a sense of discovery and reflection.

Dr. Jason Abram serves as both catalyst and anchor, his presence influencing the trajectory of every character while remaining enigmatic and morally complex. Geezer's storytelling emphasizes the importance of interpretation, questioning, and dialogue, making this a book well-suited for thoughtful discussion in book clubs or academic circles.

Miigiwewin: (The Gift) is ideal for readers who enjoy novels that combine intellectual challenge with compelling character arcs. With its layered plots, philosophical depth, and intricate narrative structure, this is a book that will leave readers contemplating its mysteries long after the final page. For those seeking a literary journey full of intrigue, personal transformation, and subtle puzzles, Miigiwewin delivers a richly rewarding and unforgettable experience.

Sacred Ashes
By T.D. Amber

T.D. Amber's Sacred Ashes: The Flames of Wisdom is a profoundly intimate and evocative work that invites readers to explore the hidden depths of emotion, resilience, and self-discovery. In this poetic journey, Amber captures the moments when silence feels heavier than words and when healing is not about illumination, but about fire—the transformative, purifying kind that burns away what no longer serves us.

The book is structured like a series of personal journal entries, blending reflective essays with moments of fiction that feel intensely real. Through these pages, Amber explores universal themes of identity, purpose, inner child healing, and spiritual awakening. Each entry is both a confession and a mirror, providing a space for readers to confront their own grief, unspoken struggles, and moments of quiet courage. There is a raw honesty in her writing that makes even the most private of emotions accessible, reminding readers that they are not alone in their journey.

What makes Sacred Ashes especially compelling is the way it reframes pain and struggle. Amber does not promise an easy path to enlightenment or a magical cure for emotional wounds. Instead, she shows that darkness itself can be sacred, that our own spark is often the light we seek. This nuanced perspective challenges readers to see suffering not as something to escape, but as a source of strength, wisdom, and transformation.

Through her reflective and poetic voice, Amber guides the reader to sit with discomfort, recognize resilience, and embrace the slow, often non-linear process of personal growth. The essays touch on divine timing, the weight of unseen emotional burdens, and the subtle, breath-by-breath unfolding of spiritual awakening.

Sacred Ashes: The Flames of Wisdom is a companion for anyone navigating life's complexities—whether struggling to be understood, seeking meaning in quiet moments, or yearning for a deeper connection to themselves and the divine. Amber's words meet readers where they are, offering both comfort and challenge. This is a work that lingers long after the last page, a reminder that the fire within us is not to be feared—it is to be honored, embraced, and trusted.

For those ready to face the sacred fire of their own inner world, Sacred Ashes is an essential, transformative read.

Deadly Vision
By T.D. Severin

Deadly Vision is a high-stakes, gripping medical thriller that masterfully blends cutting-edge technology, political intrigue, and human drama. T.D. Severin takes readers deep into the world of medical innovation, where a single breakthrough can alter the course of life—and death. At the center is Dr. Taylor Abrahms, a brilliant researcher whose experimental fusion of virtual reality, artificial intelligence, and microsurgery—the Virtual Heart Project (VHP)—allows him to enter a virtual recreation of a patient's beating heart and perform critical, life-saving surgery. The concept alone is thrilling, but Severin layers it with tension, suspense, and a keen awareness of the real-world implications of scientific progress.

The novel excels at portraying both the promise and peril of advanced technology. Taylor is not only contending with the technical challenges of his groundbreaking work but also with the political and social pressures that surround modern medicine. In a health care system teetering on the edge of crisis, his research becomes a lightning rod for controversy. Warring factions within the medical establishment, politicians, and other vested interests are willing to sabotage, discredit, and even kill to prevent the success of the VHP. Severin's narrative captures this turbulent environment with precision, making the stakes feel immediate and dangerously real.

Beyond the technological and political intrigue, Deadly Vision is deeply human. Taylor's personal journey—from a troubled past to a determined professional fighting for the lives of patients and the integrity of his work—anchors the story in emotion. The novel is populated with well-drawn characters whose loyalties, ambitions, and vulnerabilities heighten the suspense and add depth to the plot. Readers are kept on edge as the threats escalate, from career sabotage to outright murder, all while the ticking clock of a looming Presidential election adds urgency to every decision.

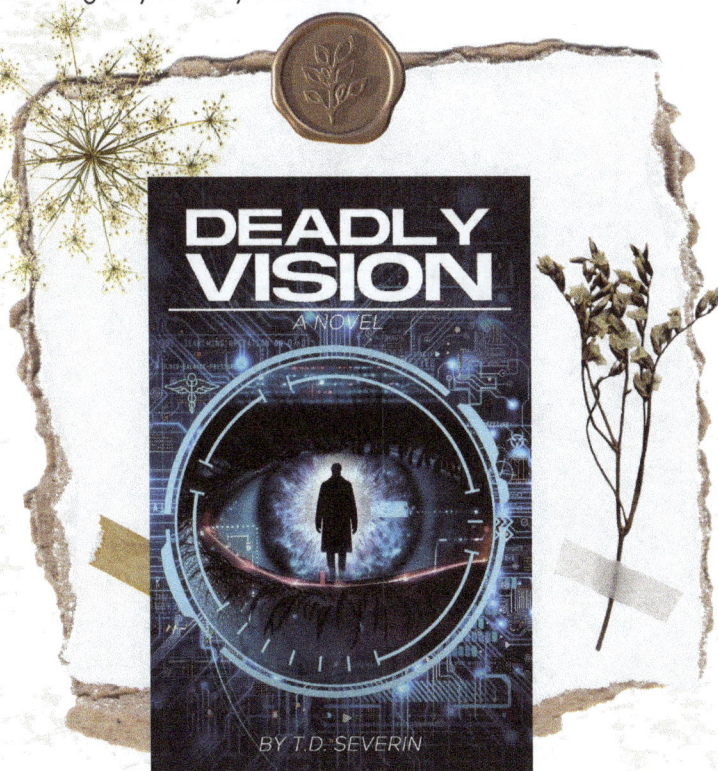

Severin writes with authority, skillfully combining medical detail, virtual reality mechanics, and psychological tension into a cohesive and thrilling narrative. Deadly Vision is not just a story of innovation and intrigue—it is a meditation on ethics, ambition, and the costs of progress. Fans of techno-thrillers, medical suspense, and high-concept thrillers will find themselves engrossed from the first page to the final, pulse-pounding climax.

Deadly Vision is an electrifying, intelligent, and deeply satisfying read that leaves you questioning what's possible in medicine, technology, and the human spirit.

23

www.ingramcontent.com/pod-product-compliance
Lightning Source LLC
Chambersburg PA
CBHW081543120626
46550CB00009B/2842